D0175069

Nature Basics

Natural and Human-Made

by Carol K. Lindeen

Consulting Editor: Gail Saunders-Smith, PhD

Consultant: Sandra Mather, PhD
Professor Emerita of Geology and Astronomy
West Chester University, Pennsylvania

Capstone press®

Mankato, Minnesota

Pebble Books are published by Capstone Press,
151 Good Counsel Drive, P.O. Box 669, Mankato, Minnesota 56002.
www.capstonepress.com

1 2 3 4 5 6 12 11 10 09 08 07

Library of Congress Cataloging-in-Publication Data
Lindeen, Carol, 1976–
  Natural and human-made / by Carol K. Lindeen.
  p. cm.—(Pebble Books. Nature basics)
  Includes bibliographical references and index.
  ISBN-13: 978-1-4296-0001-9 (hardcover)
  ISBN-10: 1-4296-0001-2 (hardcover)
  ISBN-13: 978-1-4296-2889-1 (softcover pbk.)
  ISBN-10: 1-4296-2889-8 (softcover pbk.)
  1. Materials—Juvenile literature. 2. Natural resources—Juvenile literature. 3.
Synthetic products—Juvenile literature. I. Title. II. Series.
TA403.2.L56 2008
620.1'1—dc22   2006101952

Summary: Simple text and photographs present natural and human-made resources.

Note to Parents and Teachers

The Nature Basics set supports national science standards related
to earth and life science. This book describes and illustrates natural
and human-made resources. The images support early readers in
understanding the text. The repetition of words and phrases helps
early readers learn new words. This book also introduces early
readers to subject-specific vocabulary words, which are defined
in the Glossary section. Early readers may need assistance to read
some words and to use the Table of Contents, Glossary, Read More,
Internet Sites, and Index sections of the book.

Table of Contents

Natural and Human-Made

You use resources every day.
Some resources are
natural, like sand.
Some resources are
human-made, like plastic.

Plant Resources

Wood is a natural resource.
It comes from trees.

People use wood
to make houses.
Houses are human-made.

Cotton is a
natural resource.
Cotton grows on plants.

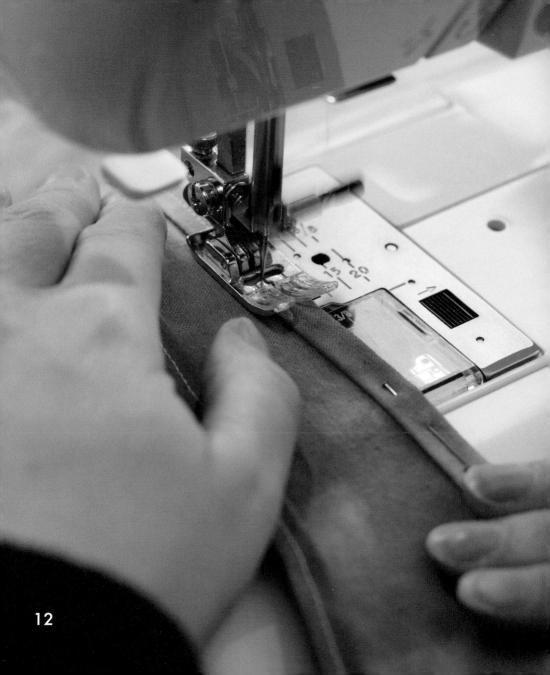

People make clothes
from cotton.
Clothes are human-made.

In the Ground

Sand is a natural resource.
It's found on the ground.

People make glass
from sand and
other materials.
Glass bottles are
human-made.

Oil is a natural resource.
A machine pumps oil
from under the ground.
People make plastic
from oil.

What else is
found in nature?
What else is
human-made?

Glossary

material—what something is made of, or can be made from

natural—something that is found in nature or made by nature; natural things are the way they are without being changed or made by humans.

plastic—a strong, lightweight material that can be made into different shapes

resource—something that can be used to fulfill a need or a want

Read More

Royston, Angela. *Natural and Man-Made.* My World of Science. Chicago: Heinemann Library, 2003.

Stille, Darlene R. *Natural Resources: Using and Protecting Earth's Supplies.* Exploring Science. Minneapolis: Compass Point Books, 2005.

Internet Sites

FactHound offers a safe, fun way to find Internet sites related to this book. All of the sites on FactHound have been researched by our staff.

Here's how:

1. Visit *www.facthound.com*
2. Choose your grade level.
3. Type in this book ID **1429600012** for age-appropriate sites. You may also browse subjects by clicking on letters, or by clicking on pictures and words.
4. Click on the **Fetch It** button.

FactHound will fetch the best sites for you!

Index

Word Count: 107
Grade: 1
Early-Intervention Level: 16

Editorial Credits
Erika L. Shores, editor; Ted Williams, designer; Jo Miller, photo researcher

Photo Credits
Corbis/First Light, 6; Lester Lefkowitz, 16
Dreamstime/Andrew Penner, 18; Andrew Ward, 14; Bartproduction, 20; Stuartkey, 12
iStockphoto/Jim Kane, 8
Shutterstock/Elena Elisseeva, cover (tree); Jodi Hutchison, 10; Mike Tolstoy/photobank.kiev.ua, cover (book); N Joy Neish, 4; Shawn Pecor, 1